101 Ways To Increase Your Wealth

101 Ways To Increase Your Wealth

Deborah Stefaniak

iUniverse, Inc.
New York   Lincoln   Shanghai

101 Ways To Increase Your Wealth

Copyright © 2005 by Deborah Stefaniak

iUniverse books may be ordered through booksellers or by contacting:

iUniverse
2021 Pine Lake Road, Suite 100
Lincoln, NE 68512
www.iuniverse.com
1-800-Authors (1-800-288-4677)

ISBN-13: 978-0-595-35173-2 (pbk)
ISBN-13: 978-0-595-79872-8 (ebk)
ISBN-10: 0-595-35173-5 (pbk)
ISBN-10: 0-595-79872-1 (ebk)

Printed in the United States of America

1.
One

Consider online banking with free e-pay. Saves the cost of stamps, envelopes and time.

2.
Two

Take advantage of dividend credit cards. Credit cards that pay 5% back on groceries and gas; 1% on purchases. Charging all your monthly expenses and paying it off at the end of the month will entitle you to a bigger check back in the mail.

3.
Three

Consider purchasing a home and/or property. Real Estate increases in value 4-5% per year. With only $10,000 down on a property for $100,000 you could earn $5,000 back the first year alone.

4.
Four

Consider purchasing a rental property as additional income.

5.
Five

Consider refinancing to a lower interest rate.

6.
Six

Consider interest only financing on investment property.

7.
Seven

Cut out weekly coupons and use them in conjunction with sale ads run by your local grocer.

8.
Eight

Watch sale ads and stock up on
nonperishable items.

9.
Nine

Take advantage of sales incentives such as 10% off total purchases when opening credit.

10.
Ten

Take advantage of rebates offered on product purchases.

11.
Eleven

Look into group auto and home insurance through a local credit union.

12.
Twelve

Consider automatic payment deductions when available with discounts to lower costs.

13.
Thirteen

Take advantage of bank incentives, such as a $25 bonus on opening new checking accounts.

14.
Fourteen

Look online for printable coupons before shopping.

15.
Fifteen

Look into state and federally governed assistance for education, veterans, nursing home care, heating credits, property tax credits and disabilities.

16.
Sixteen

Take advantage of after tax Roth-IRA contributions.

17.
Seventeen

Take advantage of any employer-sponsored 401K programs-contributing the maximum amount your employer matches.

18.
Eighteen

Take responsibility for any debt you have.
You are the one in control of your life.
Only you can create debt. Make your
choices wisely.

19.
Nineteen

Know that you deserve wealth in your life.
Believe it.

20.
Twenty

Be open to receiving wealth in your life.
Sometimes our subconscious patterning
makes us turn away from wealth, like
feelings of unworthiness.

21.
Twenty One

Give of your time, energy, or wealth to others with no "conditions" on receiving something back. The "universe" gives back what is put out.

22.
Twenty Two

Know that only you create your future. Create good thoughts and deeds about what you want that future to hold.

23.
Twenty Three

Try not to worry about money. Know that whatever happens, you'll always be OK.

24.
Twenty Four

Plan for abundance. Know that it is God's plan to give it to you.

25.
Twenty Five

Consider opening a service related
business, taking advantage of deductible
expenses, such as mileage on your
automobile, BEFORE paying taxes.

26.
Twenty Six

Consider investing in municipal bonds
that earn tax free dollars.

27.
Twenty Seven

Think in terms of how money can work for you, instead of you working for it.

28.
Twenty Eight

Always buy low or in a down market. Take advantage of a low stock market, or slow housing sales.

29.
Twenty Nine

Leverage assets against acquiring more assets. For example, use equity in your home to purchase additional investment property. The interest on your main home that you will pay additionally is deductible.

30.
Thirty

Know what assets are—boats and cars are not real assets. Consider assets that appreciate in value, not decrease.

31.
Thirty One

Don't let fear or emotion make your
financial choices.

32.
Thirty Two

See a world of opportunity, not a world with limits.

33.
Thirty Three

Be mindful that when you feel you have nothing to lose, you are free to make choices. It's only our fear of losing something that impedes our progress.

34.
Thirty Four

Realize there really is no real security—financial and physical security is only an illusion. Our real security lies within us.

35.
Thirty Five

If you've filed for bankruptcy or created a lot of debt, don't torture yourself. Everyone makes mistakes; it's how we learn. Learn not to do it again.

36.
Thirty Six

Let the opinions of others and your financial future fall by the wayside. Keep Einstein's quote in mind:
"Great spirits often encounter violent opposition from mediocre minds."

37.
Thirty Seven

Consider creating a website including online links to affiliate stores that pay you when the link is used.

38.
Thirty Eight

Make lunch instead of buying one.

39.
Thirty Nine

Car pool with someone to work, workout
or go to a special function.

40.
Forty

If your home is paid for, consider a reverse mortgage scheduling monthly payments to you from the equity of your home. (for 65 and older)

41.
Forty One

Consider publishing intellectual property (things you are knowledgeable about) to collect royalty payments. Many publishers are available now online to self publish material easily.

42.
Forty Two

Plan for tax season throughout the year instead of last minute. Documenting mileage, donations and other tax related expenses.

43.
Forty Three

Have a garage sale, selling all home and personal items you haven't used in the last year or two.

44.
Forty Four

Knowledge is power—explore all local, state and federal incentives at your local library.

45.
Forty Five

Pay off credit cards every month.

46.
Forty Six

Eat dinner at home.

47.
Forty Seven

Buy generic prescriptions.

48.
Forty Eight

Consolidate debt into one line of credit.

49.
Forty Nine

Set up a personal budget and stick to it.

50.
Fifty

Sign up on the net for free offers like baby formula and new product lines.

51.
Fifty One

Compare phone companies and rates.

52.
Fifty Two

Consider budget payments through your local utility company.

53.
Fifty Three

Consider using a phone card for long distance calls.

54.
Fifty Four

Direct deposit a set amount of money into your savings account each month to force savings.

55.
Fifty Five

Collect all change in a jar—deposit into savings account every month.

56.
Fifty Six

Put the money you save with coupons into an interest bearing account.

57.
Fifty Seven

Increase your personal sense of wealth by fixing and caring for those things around you—squeaky doors, something that needs paint, etc.

58.
Fifty Eight

Attracting money is psychological—think you are rich. If you had all the money you desired you wouldn't want ½ of what you want today. If you feel you're deprived, you'll always want. Do what's necessary to abandon feelings of deprivation.

59.
Fifty Nine

Remember, it's not how much you make but what you do with what you make that will get you to your goal.

60.
Sixty

Buy clothing on sale or clearance at the end of the season.

61.
Sixty One

Re-use gift bags/paper.

62.
Sixty Two

Appreciate all you have; good health, a
roof over your head, children…

63.
Sixty Three

Know what you earn and "exactly" where it goes each month—adjust accordingly.

64.
Sixty Four

Borrow books or movies from your local library instead of buying or renting them.

65.
Sixty Five

Wealthy people are frugal people.

66.
Sixty Six

To become wealthy you must budget and
control your expenses.

67.
Sixty Seven

To stay wealthy you must budget and control your expenses.

68.
Sixty Eight

You are not what you drive—why pay large amounts for automobiles when you can pay smaller amounts to obtain the same thing—a form of transportation.

69.
Sixty Nine

A physically fit individual works at it—To be financially fit, you must work at it as well.

70.
Seventy

Work toward becoming financially independent. Know that you'll always have it within you to obtain that independence.

71.
Seventy One

Know that it's not your job that defines you, but what you continually put into that job on a daily basis.

72.
Seventy Two

Realize when you look at a wealthy person most times it's not because of luck, it's because of continuous attention to their finances.

73.
Seventy Three

Wealth is more than increasing cash flow monthly. Increase your assets as well. Those things that earn money simply because time is passing.

74.
Seventy Four

Minimize your yearly taxable income by investing in assets which aren't taxed until they are disposed of.

75.
Seventy Five

Take advantage of any and all deductions for tax purposes. If you don't know what they are, find out. Don't rely completely on your CPA to inform you. Arm yourself with knowledge and let the professionals advise you.

76.
Seventy Six

Don't live in a highly affluent community. Don't tempt yourself to keep up with the Jones's.

77.
Seventy Seven

Look at necessities as necessities. How much MUST you pay for these? If you purchase a box of pop tarts at Wal-Mart's for $1.67 or one at Farmer Jack for $2.25 they both end up in the same place…The toilet.

78.
Seventy Eight

Become creative in ways to save cash.
Instead of purchasing a repotted plant,
plant one yourself.

79.
Seventy Nine

Know yourself. Make sure you know what things make you feel wealthy. Is it getting your hair professionally done or going to a ball game once a month? Make sure you make allowances for those things. Three quarters of all wealth is accumulated because of secure emotional feelings of wealth.

80.
Eighty

Be mindful that wealth is not accumulated over-night, but by making choices every day.

81.
Eighty One

Do you think you can be wealthy? You are what you think.

82.
Eighty Two

There isn't anyone who hasn't had financially difficulty-Luckily, however, money is an easily renewable resource.

83.
Eighty Three

Realize your financial situation does not completely mimic someone else's. Your financial picture is completely unique to you. Treat it as such and make appropriate adjustments.

84.
Eighty Four

Operate your household finances as you would a business with income, expenses, deductions and assets.

85.
Eighty Five

Utilize friend and family plans for purchase and/or lease of new vehicles. (A-plan/Z-plan)

86.
Eighty Six

Wealth is not how much money you earn per year, it's what you build up over time.

87.
Eighty Seven

Take advantage of employer plans for education. If there isn't one, ask.

88.
Eighty Eight

Utilize community sponsored concerts, movies, etc. for entertainment.

89.
Eighty Nine

Think in terms of too many expenses,
instead of not enough income.

90.
Ninety

Think of yourself as your favorite charity.

91.
Ninety One

Try not to buy anything unless it's on sale
or discounted.

92.
Ninety Two

Always live BELOW your means.

93.
Ninety Three

Just because you CAN afford it, doesn't mean you have to CHOOSE to afford it.

94.
Ninety Four

The difference between the wealthy and the middle class or poor Americans is that the wealthy have the courage to move forward-when asked of many business owners today about their difference the reply is "I had nothing to lose". Remember you are your greatest asset, not your possessions.

95.
Ninety Five

Keep your financial records organized in files in a designated place.

96.
Ninety Six

Work smarter, not necessarily harder.

97.
Ninety Seven

Never think you are limited to an amount
of income or success.

98.
Ninety Eight

Think in terms of you have no choice but to succeed. Failure is not an option.

99.
Ninety Nine

Becoming wealthy holds a fine line between feeling deprived and feeling powerful because you made the right choice.

100.
One Hundred

Don't let advertisement pull you in, or your own mind by telling you you deserve this or that. Of course you deserve it, but do you choose to have it based on your current financial situation?

101.
One Hundred and One

If you find it difficult to pay off credit cards, put them away. Pay cash for everything.

978-0-595-35173-2
0-595-35173-5

www.ingramcontent.com/pod-product-compliance
Lightning Source LLC
Chambersburg PA
CBHW030857180526
45163CB00004B/1607